The Novello Book of Carols

The Novello
Book of Carols

compiled and edited by
William Llewellyn

Novello

London and Sevenoaks

to my family
and in our affectionate remembrance of
Warren Green

A M D G

Registered office, trade orders, and hire library:
Borough Green, Sevenoaks, Kent, TN15 8DT tel: 0732 883261
Showroom, editorial, retail sales, and mail order:
8 Lower James Street, London, W1R 4DN tel: 01-734 8080

Part One Cat. No. 05 0046 ISBN 0 85360 125 9

Part Two Cat. No. 05 0047 ISBN 0 85360 126 7

Complete Cat. No. 05 0048 ISBN 0 85360 127 5

Cover illustration *I Re Magi* (S. Apollinare Nuovo, Ravenna)
© Scala/Firenze Reproduced by permission

Cover design by Malcolm Harvey Young FSIAD, MSTD

Contents

Introduction

When I was invited to produce suggestions for a comprehensive new Christmas carol collection, I was delighted to be able to draw on over 35 years' experience of organizing and directing Carol Concerts and Services. Having had to produce many arrangements of my own to suit many varied choral and instrumental demands – both amateur and professional – my initial file of ideas grew rapidly and this Novello Book of 90 Carols is the result.

16 carols and a further 39 arrangements are published here for the first time.

Carols from France, Holland, Germany, Italy, Czechoslovakia, and Canada, are included, and the three carols from Spain I obtained from Snr Enrique Ribo following a concert tour to Barcelona with the Linden Singers. Three of my own arrangements were written in Italy, and a visit to Ravenna inspired the idea for the cover illustration.

69 carols are suitable for unaccompanied singing; the Index shows this. Further, it is often useful to have readily available alternative settings – in mood, style, length, or scoring – of the same words, and 14 of these are included. The provision of Performing Notes is indicated by *PN* at the head of the music where applicable.

The book runs mainly in alphabetical order under first lines of English text, but we have made a few changes to try to keep repeated sections on facing pages and to avoid awkward turns forward or back.

Orchestral parts and full scores for 24 of the carols are obtainable on hire; details of the orchestrations, and much other useful information, will be found in the comprehensive Index at the end. This Novello Book of Carols (NBC) is also the parent book for The Novello Junior Book of Carols (NJBC) which contains 21 pieces from it. The arrangements, all compatible with NBC, have Chime Bars, School Percussion, two Melody Parts (each in C & B flat), Guitar chords, Bass Line, and simplified Piano. They make possible joint Concerts and Services with Schools and Adult Choirs; the full orchestral scores include all the school parts.

I am most grateful to all musical contributors: to James Woodhouse, Headmaster of Lancing College, for his skill in finding words which create so successfully atmosphere, sound, and meaning: to my colleague, Robin Totton, for his help with the Catalan texts: and especially to Robin Langley, Publisher to Novello & Company, for his acute perception and for his untiring interest and industry; without him, and Leslie Ellis with the expert team of technical staff, this book would never have come into being.

Charterhouse, 1986   William Llewellyn

Performing Notes

The carols are listed alphabetically under first lines

NO.   PAGE

1   1
2   2 } *A babe is born.* Each version lilts gently, with a considerable dynamic range overall, and some freedom in the unison refrains. With four voices only, omit Alto 1 and Bass 1 in the last few bars of each version.

4   6   *A little child there is yborn.* This should be taken at a steady pace so that all the quavers can be articulated – they should be crisp and detached, not smooth. It will go very well at ♩. = 92, but could be sung faster, up to ♩. = 104.

6   14   *Ancient prophets first foretold him.* This is undoubtedly a March, and the men should sound like a brass band; a good 'm' at the end of each 'Fum' will help to make the effect. The upper voices are also part of the marching procession – perhaps as children running and dancing round the band as it marches through the streets.

5   9   *As I walked down the road.* The humming accompaniment moves serenely throughout the opening. The word 'Star' (bar 26) can form a real climax, and can be matched in exhilaration by the word 'shining'.

10　22　*As Joseph was a-walking.* Serene and dignified. Verses 2 and 4 may have different soloists. The 'Mm' may have half-closed lips if this suits the acoustics.

7　16　*Away in a manger.* Even-sounding throughout, with no *crescendi* or *rallentandi* to disturb the gentle flow, and with no hint of pauses between verses. In contrast to this, the final humming surges and grows, before receding to the very soft finish.

8　18　*Blessed be he that cometh.* The 'Ah' at the beginning of each section starts confidently and then 'makes room' for the hints of plainsong which it supports. The rhythmic pulse of the Refrain makes a good contrast.

75　229　*Born in the night.* The words tell you precisely the expression needed. The layout here is explained under carol 74, p.viii, 'The First Nowell'. 'Born in the night' also sounds well between verses of 'Hark! the herald angels sing' — use two verses of 'Born in the night' each time; either transpose the carol down (to F), or up (to A flat).

9　20　*Christmas is coming.* This can have real outdoor carol style. Walford Davies once explained that in bars 5 and 6 ('hat＿＿＿') the old man is poking his hat at the passers-by. There is a chance of a spectacular *crescendo* at the end of bar 13. The traditional tune at the end will take a rustic, almost clumsy, treatment with the quavers heavier than usual. And the final unison E flat can really ring.

14　30　*De Virgin Mary had a baby boy.* Plenty of West Indian swing, and a sense of good humour can emerge. 'Duh', not 'Dee'. The dynamic contrasts should be large.

13　29　*Ding-dong, ding.* There is an alternative 'Rondo Route' through this carol and it balances well. Sing straight through the whole page with only the first set of words; straight through again, but with the second set of words; finish with the opening line. The words "'tis no fable" sound well sung very softly, as a one-bar aside.

15　34　*Ding dong! merrily on high (i).* To avoid the usual trap of 'Hosanna-rin excelsis' I asked the choir to add a rest, and the 5/4 time seemed to follow naturally.

17　37　*Donkey plod and Mary ride.* This is adapted from Eric Thiman's unison song, 'The Path to the Moon'. The carol-like quality of the tune made me look for suitable words; these by Timothy Dudley-Smith might easily have been written specially for this tune.

19　44　*Dormi Jesu. (ii).* Very calm and serene, with a feeling of a tune in each of the three parts: the cadences all have major triads and there is an opportunity for beautiful, glowing chords.

22　50　*God rest you merry, gentlemen.* This should be full of *bonhomie* and energy. The last few bars should be taken by storm.

20　46　*Hark, the herald angels sing.* Mendelssohn's 'Festgesang' (scored for male chorus and brass, and originally having no connection with Christmas) supplies the opening fanfare. The barring is his also.

21　49　*Hodie, hodie Christus natus est.* This can make an excellent start for a Carol Service or Concert. There are two possible endings to suit the keys of the carol or hymn following.

23　57　*How soft, upon the ev'ning air.* Many pieces of music have one bar or one section which suggests the speed appropriate for the whole. Here it is the bar of 'See how he sleeps'; this has a hint of both repose and movement. If this bar is at the right speed for the acoustic of the place in which you are singing, the whole will sound good.

24　60　*Hushaby low.* The chorus should be very restrained throughout, and particularly when accompanying the soprano at the beginning. Here the solo voice should be thrown into relief as though the Madonna were illuminated by a single candle in a darkened room.

25　63　*Hush you, my baby.* At bar 69 the plural word SOLOISTS asks for a soprano voice and a man's voice together. You could use more than one of each voice, but each octave should be there. It would be possible to sing the whole carol to the music of verse 2.

26　66　*I'm a-ridin' to Bethlehem.* The trotting horse ('Troc-a-tron') approaches, goes past, and away, all in a few seconds. The hard 'c' clicks in each bar, the quaver (-a-) has its own energy and the 'n' of 'tron' must be heard clearly. Though the tune comes from Czechoslovakia, you may like to try a touch of mid-Western accent. At the end of the piece no hint of slowing, but simply sounding further away until out of earshot. Your own tempo will depend on the two words 'trot quickly' and how well they sound in your acoustic.

29　76　*In the bleak mid-winter (i).* This may be sung very thoughtfully: in verse 3 (. . .'thronged the air'), the heavenly celebrations should be very loud; the singers then sing very softly without any break so that the next words 'but only his mother' are 'discovered' as the loud phrase dies away.

30　80　*In the bleak mid-winter (ii).* Verse 3 can be very effective with solo soprano accompanied by humming choir. The parts for strings and wind can be used as interludes between the sung verses.

28a　72　
28b　74　*In this most joyful night.* This arrangement of a most evocative tune is never loud — the intensity of the notes is carried up to the ends of phrases more than in our own English tradition; this brings out the elusive quality of the song.

31　81　*In thy mother's arms.* I found this lullaby in Rome and have used it frequently. The soloist sings gently above the rocking accompaniment. A little extra weight in the last bar (C flat) for the choir will help the finish, but the general mood never changes.

33　86　*I saw three ships (ii).* When John Wilson asked me to make an arrangement of this I asked, 'Which of the two well-known tunes shall I use?' His answer was 'Both!' It is quite easy to run the two different tunes at your own chosen speeds; the last few bars should be quite fast and almost 'thrown away', with the speed maintained to the final bar.

34　89　*I sing of a maiden.* Serene, using the simple resonances of the chords. With four voices only, omit Bass 1 in bars 10 and 10a.

35　90　*Jerusalem rejos for joy.* There is a great deal of atmosphere here with majesty and mystery combined, and possibilities of rich texture and colouring. 'Ch' is pronounced as in Scottish 'loch'; 'Jerusalem' and 'josit' each have a hard 'j'.

38　99　*Joy to the world (ii).* There is so much of Handel's character in this strong tune that it seemed natural to clothe the three verses with Handelian accompaniments and interludes. There are some easily-recognisable quotations in the added parts.

39　104　*King Jesus hath a garden.* Always gentle and soothing; the hints of flutes and other instruments are obvious but always miniature. This garden is sunny and contains a great variety of colour.

43　116　*Lully, lulla (ii).* In this arrangement the refrain comes only at the beginning and at the end. As well as the 3/4 time there are sections which should be sung as if they are in 3/2 and 6/8. The 6/8 in particular should be strongly rhythmical.

45 120 *Mary's Child, so new and fair.* The contraltos rock the cradle all the time. There is an echo, shown by the figures I and II, implicit in the tune (and in James Woodhouse's words). You may obtain this echo effect by distance or you may create it from within the choir. There is a real climax, but the piece is always intimate, starting almost imperceptibly and fading away to nothing at the end.

44a 118 ⎫
44b 119 ⎬ *Mary, Mother of God's dear child.* Very busy and energetic. The accents on 'Oh' in contralto, tenor, and bass can be featured. Verse 3 can be extremely quiet, with a real contrast when the *ff* final verse comes. In Spain they sing the last few bars so loudly and triumphantly that you forget your fears about waking the baby.

50 140 *Nowell, Nowell, Who is there?* Plenty of accent and robust quavers all through both the refrains and the tune sections; the final 'Nowell' should be flung out as a challenge.

53 156 *Now is Christemas ycome.* Sing buoyantly with much rhythmic verve. The repeated chords (as in bar 7) should be very full, but also clear and precise. The quavers after the ties (e.g. 'fere' in bar 10) have no length, and so the final consonant comes on the beat.

55 164 *O come, all ye faithful.* If you do not wish to sing verse 6 ('born this happy morning') you can use the setting of it for any other verse (though you will probably wish to make it your final one).

57 170 *O magnum misterium.* Each 'choir' can be replaced by an organ or by an accompanying group. Parts are available on hire for brass instruments. The characteristic richness of the writing will still be heard. The triple-time 'Alleluia' should sound very lively and buoyant.

59 184 *Once in royal David's city.* The traditional treatment of the opening verse as a solo may, of course, be adopted. For unaccompanied use, the words of verse 6 may be sung to the A.H. Mann setting on the opposite page.

60 186 *O my dear heart (ii).* A third verse, hummed *pp*, helps to carry the carol's special serenity.

62 195 *Past three o'clock (ii).* This may be performed in two different ways: you may sing the whole piece, or simply bars 32-120. This arrangement is a reminder that these are the London Waits, with the watchman calling the time as the clock chimes − no-one heeds him; and the next section is slow, with distant carol singers approaching. At bar 32 the singers have arrived; keep this part bright and lively, bringing out each carol tune as it comes. In the 'Good King Wenceslas' section, one (at most two) baritones sing first bass. Their voices should be heard only as a means of deepening and thickening the tenor-bass sound. An off-stage horn where marked (a hint of 'Die Meistersinger'?) can be effective. The horn player plays from the vocal score at concert pitch.

The dynamic range of a real bell is huge − a loud clang, dying away very rapidly, turning slowly into a humming sound which slowly dies away. A hard 'D' on the 'Don' will help; and you may get different bell timbres by inviting various 'bell-singers' to use a different vowel sound (French 'Din' is an example). The final bell-sound goes on for a long time and you can let it fade into the surrounding resonance.

65 204 *Rejoice lordings.* This should be sung with a great deal of word-energy, and in a very direct manner from beginning to end. The last bars give no hint that you are ending and should take the listener by surprise.

66 209 *See him born.* Think of a Gavotte, with firm accents on the first of the bar, and the piece will dance. Sing 'le diveen-enfant'. The humming should be nasal, buzzing, to imitate the sound and drone of pipes or French hurdy-gurdy.

67 212 ⎫
68 213 ⎬ *See, to us a child is born.* The antiphon effect can be obtained by using two groups, one singing the words in roman type, the other those in italics.

71 220 *Sweet was the song the Virgin sang.* Each of the three 'La-lu-la' sections is more expansive than the one before; the time-signatures indicate this.

72 223 *The angel Gabriel.* This arrangement dances just a little. It may be sung unaccompanied by ignoring the interludes and lengthening the last chord in verses 1-3.

74 228 *The first Nowell.* The descants are optional and can be used in any verse. The second descant (verse 4 onwards), with its cross-rhythm, is the more energetic in style.

To make a real finish to a Carol Service it is always possible to 'sandwich' one carol inside another. 'Born in the night' sung during 'The First Nowell' is a good example and it is printed here so that you may sing either carol separately, or follow the order of the printed pages. The opening of the unaccompanied verses must be carefully rehearsed.

If a congregation is to join in singing the special setting of the last verse, a congregational rehearsal will obviously be desirable.

76 234 *The holly and the ivy.* The solo voice may be a treble or a tenor, each singing in alternate verses. The organ may play with the choir, but it must play its own part in bars 12-15. A second group of singers, or congregation, may sing the tune of the refrain.

78 238 *There is no rose of such virtue.* There are opportunities here for matching the parts when singing together or in canon, with a beautiful and serene ending.

84 256 *Tyrle, tyrlow.* These words are pronounced as if made up of three syllables and split to sound 'ty-re-leh, ty-re-low'. The musical rhythm throughout must be

Ty-re-le,   ty-re-low

86 264 *Villagers all, this frosty tide.* This is the Carol of the Field-Mice, and a reading from Kenneth Grahame's 'The Wind in the Willows' makes a good introduction.

83 253 *What shall we give?* The speed should be set so that the semi-quavers receive considerable weight and become almost heavy. This is not a rocking carol. In the last verse the unusual long-held F sharp should be insistent until finally it becomes part of the last chord; the voices singing 'non' should do so emphatically and with intensity.

88 270 *Worship the Christ-child.* The three choirs may be three quartets and the canon will sound well if the groups are spaced apart. The organisation is very simple; each choir enters as soon as the previous one reaches the asterisk. Thus each choir sings through each verse once (the same music three times) and then adds the short Coda (here called 'Verse 4'). Performed in this way, Choir 1 begins alone for the first bar-and-a-half and Choir 3 finds itself singing the Coda alone at the finish. There is an obvious climax in the middle.

49. NOËL NOUVELET (ii)

Noel, sing Noel

English words by
JAMES WOODHOUSE

Traditional French carol
arranged by **IAN HUMPHRIS**

50. SIR CHRISTEMAS

Nowell, Nowell, Who is there?

Words 15th century

ROBIN WELLS

for Cumnor Choral Society

51. ALL AND SOME (ii)

Nowell sing we

Words 15th century

JOHN BYRT

[1] by [2] favour [3] bestowed

¹ misery ² enforce
*The humming can be with open or closed lips, according to the balance of the voices.

out of dis-ease he did__ us dight:__ Both all__ and some, both all __ and some.

No - well sing we,_____ No - well sing

Puer na - tus to us __ was sent, To bliss us bought, fro bale[1]__ us blent,[2]

we, No - well,_____ No - well,_____

And else to woe we had__ y-went, and else to woe we had__ y-went:__

[1]sorrow [2]turned aside

¹ pitched

[1] guide [2] tenure

52. ALL AND SOME (iii)

Nowell sing we

Words 15th century
(adapted)

JOHN JOUBERT
Opus 58

* The small notes before the beat

Words from Musica Brittanica Vol. 4 by permission of the Royal Musical Association

sing ___ we now all and some,   for *Rex* ___ pa - ci -

- fi - cus   is   come. _____

Allegro

No - well! ___

ff

Allegro

mf

ff

53. THE GOLDEN CAROL

Now is Christemas ycome

Words 15th century
(adapted)

PAUL BENDIT

54. SANS DAY CAROL

Now the holly bears a berry

Words traditional

Cornish traditional carol
arranged by IAN HUMPHRIS

4. Now the hol - ly bears a ber - ry, as blood it is red, Then

trust we our Sa - viour, who rose from the dead: *And Ma - ry bore*

Je - sus Christ our Sa - viour for to be, And the first tree in the green - wood, it

was the hol - ly, hol - ly, hol - ly! And the first tree in the

hol - ly!
green - wood, it was the hol - ly, hol - ly, hol - ly!

hol - ly!

55. ADESTE FIDELES

O come, all ye faithful

Words 18th century
trans. FREDERICK OAKLEY and others

18th century melody probably by J.F. WADE
harmonized mainly by W.H. MONK
Verse 5 arranged by H.A. CHAMBERS
Verse 6 arranged by WILLIAM LLEWELLYN

1. O come, all ye faith - ful, Joy - ful and tri - umph - ant, O come ye, O
2. God of__ God,__ Light of__ Light,__ Lo! he ab-
3. See how the shep - herds, Summoned to his cra - dle, Leav - ing their
4. Lo! star - led chief - tains, Ma - gi, Christ a - dor - ing, Of - fer him
5.* Sing, choirs of An - gels, Sing in ex - ul - ta - tion, Sing,__ all ye
6.* Yea, Lord, we greet thee, Born this hap - py morn - ing, Je - su to

come__ ye to Beth - le - hem; Come and__ be - hold__ him,
-hors__ not the Vir - gin's womb; Ve - ry__ God,__ Be -
flocks, draw nigh with low - ly fear; We too__ will thi - ther
in - cense,__ gold,__ and myrrh; We to__ the Christ - child
ci - ti - zens of heav'n__ a - bove; Glo - ry__ to God__
thee__ be__ glo - ry given; Word of__ the Fa - ther,

Born the King of An - gels:
- got - ten, not cre - a - ted:
Bend our joy - ful foot - steps:
Bring our hearts' o - bla - tions:
In the high - est:
Now in flesh ap - pear - ing:

O come, let us a - dore him, O come, let us a -

- dore him, O come, let us a - dore him,__ Christ__ the Lord!

*for extended versions of these verses see pp. 165-167.

for the Inner London Education Authority Central
Young Musicians' Chamber Choir

56. O LEAVE YOUR SHEEP

English words by
ALICE RALEIGH

Traditional French tune
Quittez pasteurs
arranged by IAN HUMPHRIS

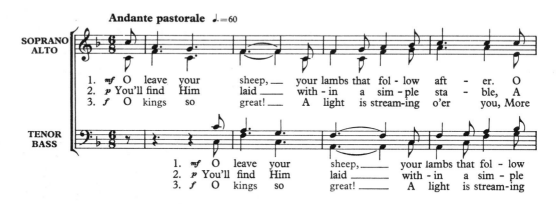

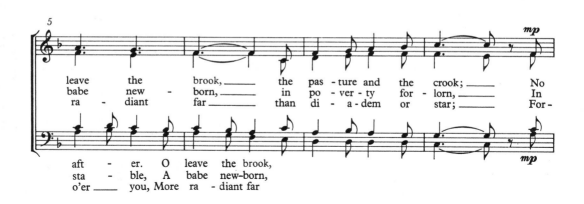

shep-herds seek your goal! ____ Your Lord, ____ your Lord, ____ your
search the world for you: ____ 'Tis He, ____ 'tis He, ____ 'tis
won-der shall be told: ____ Bring myrrh, ____ bring myrrh, ____ bring

Lord who com-eth to ____ con - sole! ____ Your Lord, ____ your
He, 'tis He the shep - herd ___ true! ____ 'Tis He, ____ 'tis
myrrh, bring frank - in - cense ___ and ___ gold! ____ Bring myrrh, ____ bring

Lord, ____ your Lord who com - eth to ____ con - sole! ____
He, ____ 'tis He, 'tis He the shep - herd ___ true! ____
myrrh, ____ bring myrrh, bring frank - in - cense ___ and ___ gold! ____

57. O MAGNUM MISTERIUM

GIOVANNI GABRIELI
edited by WILLIAM LLEWELLYN

58. BALULALOW (i)

Paraphrase of Luther's
Vom Himmel Hoch in
Ane Compendious Buik of Godly
and Spiritual Sangis, 1567

O my dear heart

RICHARD RODNEY BENNETT

Piacevole ♪ = 112

SOPRANO

ALTO

O my dear heart, young Je - su sweet, Pre - pare thy cra - dle in my spreit, And I shall rock thee in my heart, And ne - ver - more from thee de - part. But I shall praise thee ev - er - more, With

song - is sweet un - to thy gloir. The knees of my heart shall I bow And sing that sweet Ba - lu - la - low.

59. ONCE IN ROYAL DAVID'S CITY

Words by
CECIL FRANCES ALEXANDER

HENRY J. GAUNTLETT
arranged by A. H. MANN
last verse arranged by ROBIN WELLS

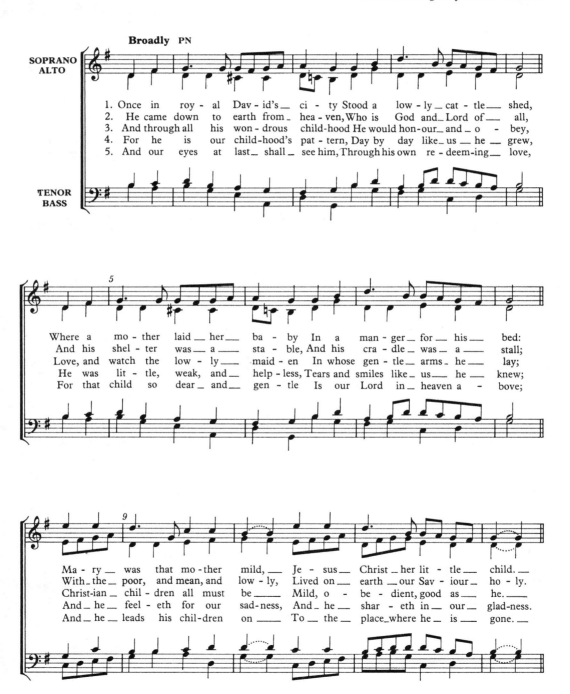

60. BALULALOW (ii)

O my dear heart

Paraphrase of Luther's
Vom Himmel Hoch in
*Ane Compendions Buik of
Godly and Spiritual Sangis*, 1567
adapted by ANTHONY PETTI

PAUL JOHNSON

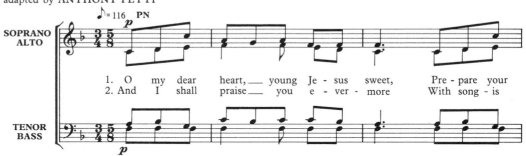

1. O my dear heart, young Jesus sweet, Prepare your
2. And I shall praise you evermore With songis

cradle in my spreit, And I shall rock you in my
sweet unto your gloir; With all my heart to you I

And nevermore from you depart.
bow, And sing that richt Balulalow.

Reprinted from *The New Catholic Hymnal* by permission of the publishers Faber Music Limited and Paul Johnson

61. THE TWELVE DAYS OF CHRISTMAS

On the First day of Christmas

Words traditional

Traditional English tune
with additions by FREDERIC AUSTIN
arranged by IAN HUMPHRIS

105 seven Swans a - swim-ming, *Quack! Quack!* five Gold

five Gold

five Gold

swim - ming, six Geese a - lay-ing,

108 Rings,

Rings,

Rings, four Call - ing Birds,

mf four Call - ing Birds, three French Hens,

poco rit. **a tempo**

Tree.

111 two Tur-tle Doves, and a Par - tridge in a Pear Tree, in a Pear Tree,

114 **S.**

A. *p leggiero*

in a Pear Tree. *La, la, la; la, la, la; la, la, la, la, la, la.*

T. *p leggiero*

in a Pear Tree. *La, la, la, la, la, la, la, la.*

SOLO
12. On the Twelfth day of Christ - mas my true love sent to me

B. *f*

Par - tridge: **THE REST** *p leggiero*
La, la, la, la, la.

62. LONDON WAITS (i)

Past three o'clock

Words by
G. R. WOODWARD
with traditional refrain

Tune *London Waits*
harmonized by
CHARLES WOOD

Past three o' clock, And a cold frost-y morn-ing; Past three a clock; Good mor-row, mas-ters all! Born is a Ba-by, Gen-tle as may be, Son of th'e-ter-nal Fa-ther su-per-nal.

2. Seraph quire singeth,
Angel bell ringeth:
Hark how they rime it,
Time it, and chime it.

3. Mid earth rejoices
Hearing such voices
Ne'ertofore so well
Carolling *Nowell.*

4. Hinds o'er the pearly
Dewy lawn early
Seek the high stranger
Laid in the manger.

5. Cheese from the dairy
Bring they for Mary,
And, not for money,
Butter and honey.

6. Light out of star-land
Leadeth from far land
Princes, to meet him,
Worship and greet him.

7. Myrrh from full coffer,
Incense they offer:
Nor is the golden
Nugget withholden.

8. Thus they: I pray you,
Up, sirs, nor stay you
Till ye confess him
Likewise, and bless him.

63. LONDON WAITS (ii)

Past three o'clock

Words by
G. R. WOODWARD
with traditional refrain

Quodlibet
arranged by WILLIAM LLEWELLYN

64. A GALLERY CAROL

Rejoice and be merry

Words traditional

Old English tune
arranged by ROBIN WELLS

1. Re-joice and be mer-ry in songs and in mirth, O praise our Re-deem-er, all mor-tals on earth. For this is the birth-day of Je-sus our King, Who brought us sal-va-tion, his prais-es we'll sing.

SOPRANOS and ALTOS

2. A hea-ven-ly vi-sion ap-peared in the sky; Vast num-bers of an-gels the Shep-herds did spy, Pro-claim-ing the birth-day of Je-sus our King, Who brought us sal-va-tion, his prais-es we'll sing.

Man.

p legato

Ped.

for Gerald Smith and the Choir of St. Dominic's

65. REJOICE LORDINGS

Words Early English

ARTHUR OLDHAM

boght   us   all   up - on   the   rood   *Su - a   mor - te   pi -*

-a.

3. For   the   tres - pass   of   A - dam   From   the   Fa - ther of

3. For   the   tres - pass   of   A - dam

66. IL EST NÉ, LE DIVIN ENFANT

See him born, the Heavenly Child

English words by
JAMES WOODHOUSE

French traditional carol
arranged by WILLIAM LLEWELLYN

67. A CHRISTMAS ANTIPHON (i)

See, to us a child is born

A Christmas Antiphon
based on Isaiah 9.6,7
TIMOTHY DUDLEY-SMITH

Tune *Lauds*
JOHN WILSON

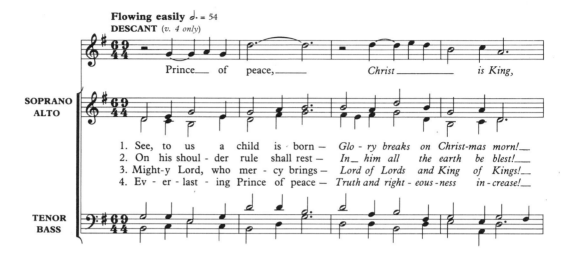

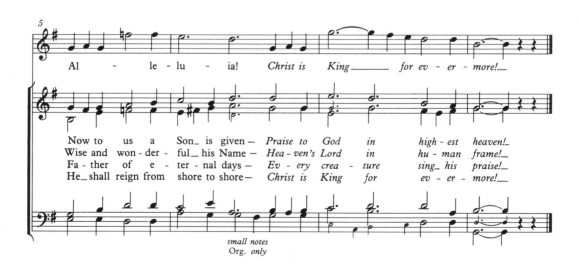

68. A CHRISTMAS ANTIPHON (ii)

See, to us a child is born

A Christmas Antiphon
based on Isaiah 9.6,7 by
TIMOTHY DUDLEY-SMITH

Tune *Lauds* by JOHN WILSON
arranged by WILLIAM LLEWELLYN

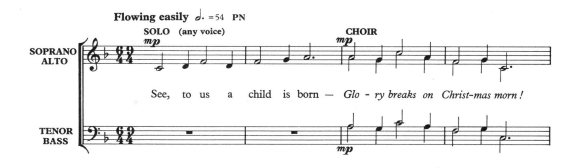

See, to us a child is born — *Glo-ry breaks on Christ-mas morn!*

Now to us a Son is given *Praise to God in high-est heaven!*

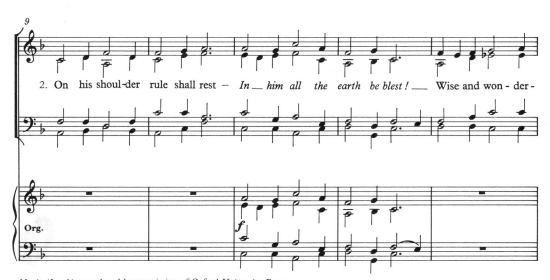

2. On his shoul-der rule shall rest — *In him all the earth be blest!* Wise and won-der-

69. STILLE NACHT

Silent night

German words by JOSEPH MOHR
English words adapted by JAMES WOODHOUSE

Melody by FRANZ GRÜBER
arranged by IAN HUMPHRIS

70. THE INFANT KING

Sing lullaby!

Words by
S. BARING-GOULD

Traditional Basque Noël
arranged by WILLIAM LLEWELLYN

1. Lul-la-by ba-by, now re-clin-ing,
2. Lul-la-by ba-by, now a-sleep-ing, *Sing lul-la-*
3. Lul-la-by ba-by, now a-doz-ing,

Sing lul-la-by!

Sing lul-la-by!

Hush, do not wake the_ In-fant_ King. An-gels are
Hush, do not wake the_ In-fant_ King. Soon_ will come
Hush, do not wake the_ In-fant_ King. Soon_ comes the

- *by!*_

watch-ing, stars are shin-ing_ O-ver the place where_ he_ is
sor-row with_ the_ morn-ing,_ Soon will come bit-ter_ grief_ and
cross, the_ nails,_ the_ pierc-ing,_ Then in the grave at last_ re-

ly - ing.
weep - ing: *Sing lul-la-by,_ Sing lul-la-by!*
- pos - ing:

for Ashtead Choral Society

71. LUTE-BOOK LULLABY

Sweet was the song the Virgin sang

Words from the Lute-Book of
WILLIAM BALLET (17th cent.)

Jeremy Thurlow

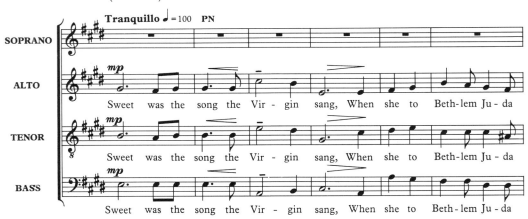

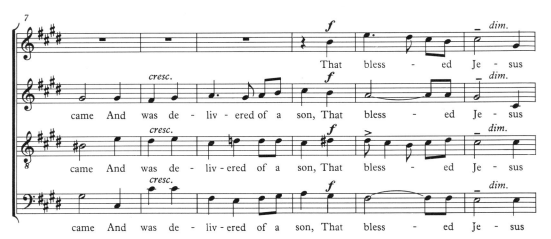

72. GABRIEL'S MESSAGE

The angel Gabriel from heaven came

Words by
S. BARING-GOULD

Basque carol
arranged by WILLIAM LLEWELLYN

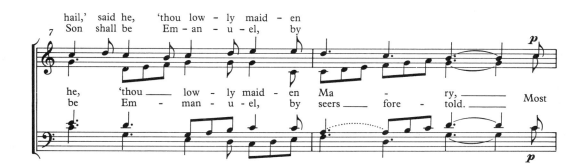

*Omit if unaccompanied.

Melody © 1961 H. Freeman & Co. Reproduced by permission of EMI Music Publishing Ltd and International Music Publications

3. Then gen-tle Ma-ry meek-ly bowed her head,___ 'To me be as it pleas-eth

God,'___ she said,___ 'My soul shall laud and mag-ni-fy his Ho-ly Name.'___

Most high-ly favoured la-dy, Glo - - ri-a! ___

* Omit if unaccompanied

73. CAROL OF THE CHRIST-CHILD

The Christ-child lay on Mary's lap

Words by
G. K. CHESTERTON

PHILIP RILEY

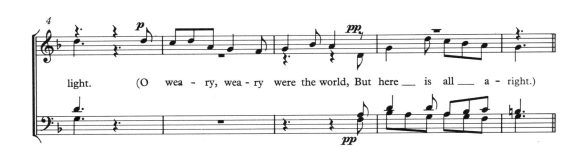

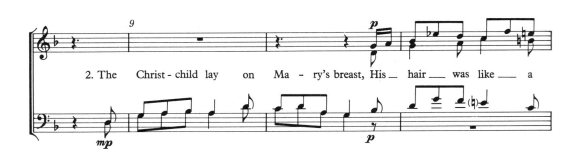

Words reproduced by permission of Miss D. Collins and J.M. Dent & Sons Ltd.

74. THE FIRST NOWELL

Traditional English carol
arranged by JOHN STAINER
descant and final verse
arranged by WILLIAM LLEWELLYN

Words traditional

for verses 4 – 6 see p.230

This layout makes possible the singing of *The First Nowell* interspersed with verses of *Mary's Child* (see Performing Notes).

75. MARY'S CHILD

Born in the night

Words by
GEOFFREY AINGER

GEOFFREY AINGER
arranged by WILLIAM LLEWELLYN

for verses 3 and 4 see p.231

This layout makes possible the singing of *Mary's Child* interspersed with verses of *The First Nowell* (see Performing Notes).

4. This star drew nigh to the north-west; O'er Beth-le-
hem it took its rest, And there it did both stop and stay Right o-ver the place where Je-sus lay:

5. Then en-ter'd in those Wise Men three, Full rev-'rent-ly up-on their knee, And of-fered there in his pres-ence Their gold and myrrh and frank-in-cense:

6.* Then let us all with one ac-cord, Sing prais-es to our heaven-ly Lord, That hath made heaven and earth of naught And with his blood man-kind hath bought:

DESCANT

No-well, No-well, No-well, No-well, No-well, No-well, No-well, No-well, No-well.

No-well, No-well, No-well, Born is the King of Is-ra-el.

* see page 232 for final verse arrangement

3. Truth of our life, Mary's Child, You tell us God is good;
4. Hope of the world, Mary's Child, You're coming soon to reign;

Prove it is true, Mary's Child, Go to your cross of wood.
King of the earth, Mary's Child, Walk in our streets again.

234

76. THE HOLLY AND THE IVY

Words traditional

Gloucestershire Folk Carol
collected by CECIL SHARP
arranged by WILLIAM LLEWELLYN

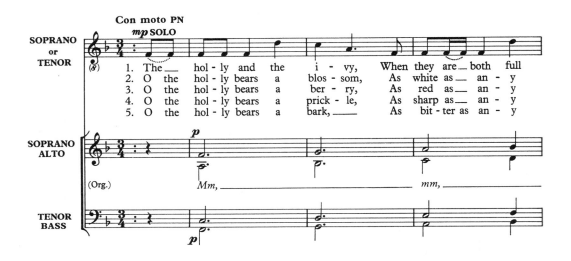

1. The __ hol - ly and the i - vy, When they are __ both full
2. O the hol - ly bears a blos - som, As white as __ an - y
3. O the hol - ly bears a ber - ry, As red as __ an - y
4. O the hol - ly bears a prick - le, As sharp as __ an - y
5. O the hol - ly bears a bark, __ As bit - ter as an - y

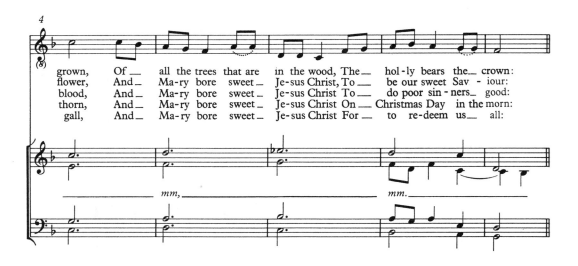

grown, Of __ all the trees that are in the wood, The __ hol - ly bears the __ crown:
flower, And __ Ma - ry bore sweet __ Je - sus Christ, To __ be our sweet Sav - iour:
blood, And __ Ma - ry bore sweet __ Je - sus Christ To __ do poor sin - ners __ good:
thorn, And __ Ma - ry bore sweet __ Je - sus Christ On __ Christmas Day in the morn:
gall, And __ Ma - ry bore sweet __ Je - sus Christ For __ to re - deem us __ all:

© Oxford University Press 1965

77. THE TREES OF THE FIELD

The oak stands fast

Words by
E. M. JAMESON

DAVID STONE

Copyright © 1957 by Boosey & Co., Ltd

78. THERE IS NO ROSE OF SUCH VIRTUE

Words Medieval

JOHN JOUBERT

79. THE SHEPHERDS' FAREWELL

Thou must leave thy lowly dwelling

Words by
PAUL ENGLAND

HECTOR BERLIOZ

80. TORCHES! (i)

Words translated
from the Galician
by J. B. TREND

JOHN JOUBERT

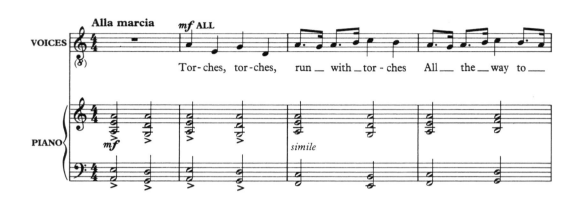

Tor-ches, tor-ches, run _ with _ tor-ches All _ the _ way to _

Beth-le-hem! Christ is born and now _ lies _ sleep-ing; Come _ and _ sing your _

song to him! Tor-ches, tor-ches, run _ with _ tor-ches All _ the _ way to _

Words from *The Oxford Book of Carols* by permission of Oxford University Press

Beth-le-hem! Christ is born and now lies sleep-ing; Come and sing your song to him!

Ah, Ro-ro, Ro-ro, my ba-by, Ah, Ro-ro, my love, Ro-ro;

Sleep you well, my heart's own dar-ling, While we sing you our Ro-ro.

Sing, my friends, and make you mer-ry, Joy and mirth and joy a-gain;

Sing, my friends, and make you mer-ry, sing, my friends, and

81. TORCHES! (ii)

Words translated
from the Galician
by J. B. TREND

JOHN JOUBERT

82. HURON CAROL

'Twas in the moon of wintertime

Attributed to Father JEAN DE BREBEUF
English words by J.E. MIDDLETON

Tune of the Huron Indians
arranged by WILLIAM LLEWELLYN

SOPRANO
ALTO

1. 'Twas in the moon of win-ter-time, when all the birds had fled, That
2. With-in a lodge of bro-ken bark, the ten-der babe was found, A

TENOR
BASS

1. 'Twas win - ter - time, _____ That
2. With-in _____ a lodge _____ his

might-y Git-chi Ma-ni-tou sent an-gel choirs in-stead. Be-
rag-ged robe of rab-bit skin en-wrapped his beau-ty round, And,

Man - i - tou _____ And
beau - ty round, _____ The

- fore their lights the stars grew dim, And wand'-ring hun-ters heard the hymn.
as the hun-ter braves drew nigh, The an-gel song rang loud and high.

wand - 'ring hun - ters heard the _____ hymn. _____
an - gel song rang loud and _____ high. _____

Je - sus your King is born, _____ Je - sus is born, in ex-cel-sis glo-ri-a.
Je - sus _____ your Je - sus is

Je - sus, Je - sus _____ is born, _____ glo - ri - a.

Words reproduced by permission of Frederick Harris Limited and their UK Agents William Elkin Music Services
© Copyright 1986 Novello & Company Limited
All Rights Reserved

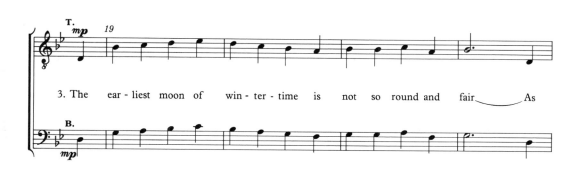

3. The ear - liest moon of win - ter - time is not so round and fair____ As

was the ring of glo - ry on that help - less in - fant there. The

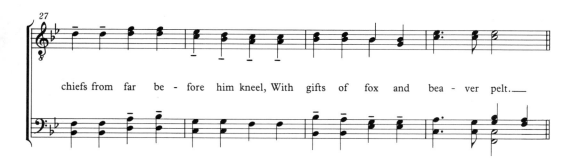

chiefs from far be - fore him kneel, With gifts of fox and bea - ver pelt.___

Je-sus your King is born, Je - sus is born,_ in ex - cel-sis glo - ri - a.

Je - sus__ your King is born,_ Je-sus is__ born,_ in ex - cel-sis glo - ri - a.

Je - sus Je - sus___ is born,___ glo - ri - a.

4. O chil-dren of the for-est free, O Sons of Ma-ni-tou, The

Ho-ly child of earth and heav'n is born to-day for you,

Come kneel be-fore the ra-diant boy, who gives you beau-ty, peace and joy.

Je-sus your King is born,— Je-sus is born,— in ex-cel-sis glo-ri-a, in ex-

Je-sus is born,

Je-sus, Je-sus is born, glo-ri-a,

glo - ri - a.

-cel-sis glo-ri-a, in ex-cel-sis glo-ri-a.

glo-ri-a,

glo-ri-a.

83. EL NOI DE LA MARE

What shall we give?

English words by
JAMES WOODHOUSE

Traditional Catalan carol
arranged by ENRIQUE RIBO

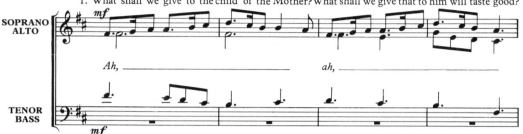

84. TYRLE, TYRLOW

Words from
Balliol MS 1536

HEALEY WILLAN

shepherds a - non _____ gan them a - spy. _____ Tyr-

- le, tyr - low, tyr - le, tyr - low! *Glo - ri - a in ex - cel - sis,* the an - gels sang, And

said that peace was pre - sent a - mong To ev - 'ry man that _____ to the faith _ would

fong.[1] _____ Tyr - le, tyr - low, tyr - le, tyr - low! The

shep - herds hied them to Bed - lem, To see that bless - ed Sun __ His beam; And

there_ they found _____ that glo - rious leme.[2] _____ Tyr-

[1] accept [2] ray

85. PUER NOBIS

Unto us is born a son

English words by
G.R. WOODWARD

Tune: *Piae Cantiones*, 1582
arranged by WILLIAM LLEWELLYN

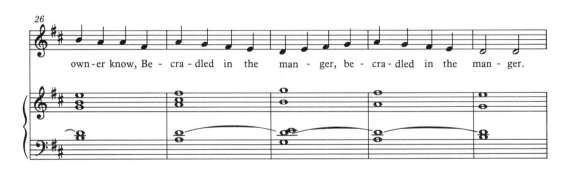

own-er know, Be - cra - dled in the man - ger, be - cra - dled in the man - ger.

TENORS and BASSES

3. This did He-rod   sore af - fray, And griev-ous - ly be - wil - der,   So he gave the

Ped.

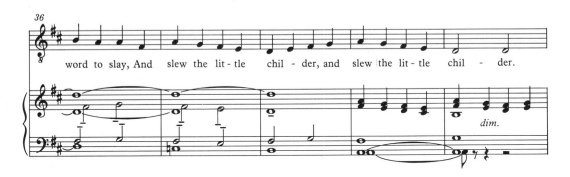

word to slay, And   slew the lit - tle   chil - der, and slew the lit - tle   chil - der.

dim.

SOPRANOS

4. Of his   love and mer - cy mild   This the Christ-mas sto - ry: And   O that Ma-ry's

Man.

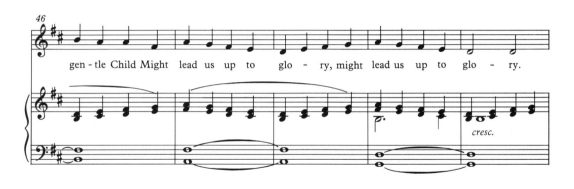

86. JOY SHALL BE YOURS IN THE MORNING

Villagers all, this frosty tide

Words by
KENNETH GRAHAME

H. FRASER-SIMSON

Copyright 1930 by Chappell & Co.

for the Linden Singers

87. THE YORKSHIRE WASSAIL

Wassail: We've been a while a-wandering

Words traditional

Yorkshire carol
arranged by IAN HUMPHRIS

3. Call/

88. CANON FOR THREE CHOIRS

Worship the Christ-child

Words by
WILLIAM LLEWELLYN

W. A. MOZART
K.348

89. WHENCE IS THAT GOODLY FRAGRANCE FLOWING? (i)

English words by
A.B. RAMSAY

French traditional carol
arranged by WILLIAM LLEWELLYN

for Farnham and Bourne Choral Society

90. WHENCE IS THAT GOODLY FRAGRANCE FLOWING? (ii)

English words by
A.B. RAMSAY

French traditional carol
arranged by ROBIN WELLS

INDEX

ABBREVIATIONS: U=Unaccompanied S=Soprano A=Alto T=Tenor B=Bass Br=Baritone Perc.=Percussion Tp=Timpani

ORCHESTRAL FORCES: Wind (2222)=2 Flutes, 2 Oboes, 2 Clarinets, 2 Bassoons; Brass (2231)=2 Horns, 2 Trumpets, 3 Trombones, 1 Tuba; Tp+2=Timpani+2 further percussion players

NO.	PAGE	U	TITLE AND FIRST LINE (both are shown)	TIME	COMPOSER OR ARRANGER	Solo	Minimum Choir	Wind	Brass	Perc.	Strings	JUNIOR BOOK (NJBC)
1	1	U	A babe is born (i)	2'15"	Robin Wells		SATB					
2	2	U	A babe is born (ii)	2'15"	Robin Wells		SATB					
67	212	U	A Christmas Antiphon (See, to us a child is born) (i)	1'30"	John Wilson		SATB					
68	213	U	A Christmas Antiphon (See, to us a child is born) (ii)	1'30"	John Wilson /W. Ll.		SATB					
3	4	U	Adam lay ybounden	1'00"	Boris Ord		SATB					
21	49	U	A Fanfare for Christmas (Hodie, hodie)	1'00"	Robin Wells		SAATB	2222	2231	Tp+2	Strings	
64	200		A Gallery Carol (Rejoice and be merry)	1'30"	Robin Wells		SATB	2222	2231	Tp+2	Strings	NJBC
4	6	U	A little child there is yborn (Susanni)	1'45"	Ronald Corp		SATB					
48	133	U	All and some (Nowell sing we) (i)	1'55"	Jeremy Thurlow		SAATTBB	1111	1111	0+3	Strings	
51	142	U	All and some (Nowell sing we) (ii)	3'35"	John Byrt	S	SSAATTBB					
52	148	U	All and some (Nowell sing we) (iii)	2'40"	John Joubert		SATB					
6	14	U	Ancient prophets first foretold him (Fum, fum, fum)	1'10"	William Llewellyn		SATTBB					NJBC
5	9	U	As I walked down the road (The little road to Bethlehem)	3'00"	Michael Head		SSAATTBB					
10	22	U	As Joseph was a-walking	1'45"	Robin Wells	S/T	SATB					
12	26		A Somerset Carol (Come all you worthy people here)	1'30"	William Llewellyn		SATB	2222	2231	Tp+2	Strings	NJBC
7	16	U	Away in a manger	2'15"	W. J. Kirkpatrick/W. Ll.	S	SSAATTBBB				Strings	
58	183	U	Balulalow (O my dear heart) (i)	1'05"	Richard R. Bennett		SSSA					
60	186	U	Balulalow (O my dear heart) (ii)	1'40"	Paul Johnson		SATB					
8	18	U	Blessed be he that cometh (Dawn Carol)	3'15"	Malcolm Williamson		SAATTB					
75	229	U	Born in the night (Mary's Child)	1'40"	Geoffrey Ainger/W. Ll.		SATTBB					NJBC

NO.	PAGE	U	TITLE AND FIRST LINE (both are shown)	TIME	COMPOSER OR ARRANGER	Minimum Choir	Solo	Wind	Brass	Perc.	Strings	JUNIOR BOOK (NJBC)
88	270	U	Canon for three choirs (*Worship the Christ-child*)	1'30"	*W. A. Mozart/W. Ll.*	[SATB]×3						
73	226	U	Carol of the Christ-child (*The Christ-child lay*)	1'30"	*Philip Riley*	SATB						
11	23	U	*Christmas Eve* (The Oxen)	2'30"	*Benjamin Britten*	SA						
9	20	U	*Christmas is coming*	1'40"	*Walford Davies*	SATB						
12	26		Come all you worthy people here (A Somerset Carol)	1'30"	*William Llewellyn*	SATB	S	2222	2231	Tp+2	Strings	NJBC
42	113	U	Coventry Carol (*Lully, lulla*) (i)	2'30"	*Kenneth Leighton*	SATBB						
43	116	U	Coventry Carol (*Lully, lulla*) (ii)	2'25"	*Ian Humphris*	SSAATTBB						
8	18	U	Dawn Carol (*Blessed be he that cometh*)	3'15"	*Malcolm Williamson*	SAATTB						
14	30	U	De Virgin Mary had a baby boy	2'20"	*William Llewellyn*	TTBB	Br	2222	2231	Tp+2	Strings	
13	29	U	Ding-dong, ding	1'30"	*G. R. Woodward*	SATB						
15	34	U	Ding dong! merrily on high (i)	2'10"	*William Llewellyn*	SATB						
16	36	U	Ding dong! merrily on high (ii)	2'00"	*H. Le Fèvre Pope*	SSA						NJBC
17	37		Donkey plod and Mary ride	4'30"	*Eric Thiman/W. Ll.*	SATB						
18	43	U	Dormi Jesu (Our Lady's Lullaby) (i)	0'45"	*Philip Riley*	SSAA						
19	44	U	Dormi Jesu (Our Lady's Lullaby) (ii)	1'30"	*Richard R. Bennett*	SSAA						
28b	74	U	El Cant des Ocells (*En veure despuntar*)	3'00"	*Enrique Ribo*	SATB						
83	253	U	El Noi de la Mare (*What shall we give?*)	1'50"	*Enrique Ribo*	SSAATTBB	S					
28b	74	U	En veure despuntar (El Cant des Ocells)	3'00"	*Enrique Ribo*	SATB	S					
6	14	U	Fum, fum, fum (*Ancient prophets first foretold him*)	1'10"	*William Llewellyn*	SAATTB						NJBC
72	223	U	Gabriel's message (*The angel Gabriel*)	2'15"	*William Llewellyn*	SATB		1200			Strings	NJBC
22	50		God rest you merry, gentlemen	2'00"	*William Llewellyn*	SSATBB		2222	2231	Tp+2	Strings	NJBC
20	46		*Hark!* the herald angels sing	3'20"	*Mendelssohn/W. Ll.*	SATB		2222	2231	Tp+2	Strings	NJBC
21	49	U	Hodie, hodie (A Fanfare for Christmas)	1'00"	*Robin Wells*	SATB		2222	2231	Tp+2	Strings	
23	57		*How soft, upon the ev'ning air*	1'40"	*Thomas Dunhill/W. Ll.*	SAATTBB		2200			Strings	

No.	Page		Title		Composer	Voicing	Solo					
82	250	U	Huron Carol ('Twas in the moon of wintertime)	1'50"	William Llewellyn	SSAATBB						
24	60	U	Hushaby low (Slumber Song of the Madonna)	2'00"	Ronald Finch	SAATTBB	S					
25	63	U	Hush you, my baby	3'10"	William Llewellyn	SSAATTBB	ST					
66	209	U	Il est né, le divin enfant (See him born)	2'00"	William Llewellyn	SSAATBB		1200			Strings	NJBC
35	90	U	Illuminare, Jerusalem (Jerusalem rejos for joy)	2'30"	Judith Weir	SSAATBB						
26	66	U	I'm a-ridin' to Bethlehem (Troc-a-tron)	0'50"	Petr Eben	SATB						
27	68	U	In dulci jubilo	3'45"	R. L. Pearsall	SATB						
29	76	U	In the bleak mid-winter (i)	3'45"	William Llewellyn	SATB						
30	80	U	In the bleak mid-winter (ii)	3'45"	Gustav Holst	SATB						
28a	72	U	In this most joyful night (The Song of the Birds)	3'00"	Enrique Ribo	SATB						
31	81	U	In thy mother's arms (Ninna-Nanna)	1'50"	D. Lavinio Virgili	SATB	A/Br	1111			Strings	NJBC
32	84	U	I saw three ships (i)	1'00"	Ian Humphris	SATB						
33	86	U	I saw three ships (ii)	2'05"	William Llewellyn	SAATTBB	TB					
34	89	U	I sing of a maiden	1'20"	Robin Wells	SATTB						
35	90		Jerusalem rejos for joy (Illuminare, Jerusalem)	2'30"	Judith Weir	SSAATBB						
36	95	U	Jesus, Jesus, rest your head	2'20"	J. J. Niles/Warrell	SATB						
86	264	U	Joy shall be yours (Villagers all, this frosty tide)	1'30"	H. Fraser-Simson	SATB						
37	98	U	Joy to the World (i)	1'30"	? G. F. Handel	SATB		2222	2231	Tp	Strings	NJBC
38	99		Joy to the World (ii)	2'00"	? G. F. Handel/W. Ll.	SATB		2222	0200	Tp	Strings	
39	104		King Jesus hath a garden	3'05"	William Llewellyn	SSAA		2221	2200	Tp+2	Strings	NJBC
40	108		Lady, I sing to thee (Our Lady and Child)	1'40"	Philip Moore	SSATB						
62	195	U	London Waits (Past three o'clock) (i)	2'00"	Charles Wood	SATB						NJBC
63	196	U	London Waits (Past three o'clock) (ii)	3'00"	William Llewellyn	SSAATBB	Br					
41	110	U	Lullay my liking	2'30"	Gustav Holst	SATB						
42	113	U	Lully, lulla (Coventry Carol) (i)	2'30"	Kenneth Leighton	SATBB	S					
43	116	U	Lully, lulla (Coventry Carol) (ii)	2'25"	Ian Humphris	SSAATTBB						
71	220	U	Lute-book Lullaby (Sweet was the song the Virgin sang)	2'15"	Jeremy Thurlow	SSAATTBB						

NO.	PAGE	U	TITLE AND FIRST LINE (both are shown)	TIME	COMPOSER OR ARRANGER	VOICES Minimum Choir	Solo	Wind	Brass	Perc.	Strings	JUNIOR BOOK (NJBC)
44a	118	U	Mary, Mother of God's dear child (Sant Josep i la Mare)	1'30"	Père Jorda	SATB						
75	229	U	Mary's Child (Born in the night)	1'40"	Geoffrey Ainger/W. Ll.	SATTBB						NJBC
45	120	U	Mary's Child, so new and fair (Rocking Carol)	1'35"	William Llewellyn	SAATTBB						NJBC
46	124	U	Mary walked through a wood of thorn	1'05"	Philip Radcliffe	SATB						
31	81	U	Ninna-Nanna (In thy mother's arms)	1'50"	D. Lavinio Virgili	SATB	A/Br					
47	126	U	Noel Nouvelet (Noël Nouvelet) (i)	3'20"	Stephen Jackson	SSAATTBB	S	2222	2230	Tp+1	Strings	
49	137	U	Noël Nouvelet (Noel, sing Noel) (ii)	2'35"	Ian Humphris	SATB						
49	137	U	Noel, sing Noel (Noël Nouvelet) (ii)	2'35"	Ian Humphris	SATB						
50	140	U	Nowell, Nowell, Who is there? (Sir Christemas)	1'05"	Robin Wells	SATBB						
48	133	U	Nowell sing we (All and some) (i)	1'55"	Jeremy Thurlow	SSAATTBB		1111	1111	0+3	Strings	
51	142	U	Nowell sing we (All and some) (ii)	3'35"	John Byrt	SSAATTBB	S					
52	148	U	Nowell sing we (All and some) (iii)	2'40"	John Joubert	SATB						
53	156	U	Now is Christemas ycome (The Golden Carol)	1'10"	Paul Bendit	SSAATTBB						
54	160	U	Now the holly bears a berry (Sans Day Carol)	1'50"	Ian Humphris	SAATTBB						
55	164	U	O come, all ye faithful	4'20"	William Llewellyn	SATB		2222	2231	Tp+3	Strings	NJBC
56	168	U	O leave your sheep	2'15"	Ian Humphris	SATB						
57	170	U	O magnum misterium	2'15"	Giovanni Gabrieli/ W. Ll.	SATB: TTBB			1210: 1021			
58	183	U	O my dear heart (Balulalow) (i)	1'05"	Richard R. Bennett	SSSA						
60	186	U	O my dear heart (Balulalow) (ii)	1'40"	Paul Johnson	SATB						
59	184	U	Once in royal David's city	5'30"	Gauntlett/Mann/Wells	SATB	S	2222	2231	Tp+3	Strings	NJBC
61	187	U	On the First day (The Twelve Days of Christmas)	3'40"	Ian Humphris	SSAATTBB	SB					NJBC
40	108	U	Our Lady and Child (Lady, I sing to thee)	1'40"	Philip Moore	SSATB						
18	43	U	Our Lady's Lullaby (Dormi Jesu) (i)	0'45"	Philip Riley	SSAA						
19	44	U	Our Lady's Lullaby (Dormi Jesu) (ii)	1'30"	Richard R. Bennett	SSAA						

No.		Page	Title	Duration	Composer/Arranger	Voices						
62	U	195	Past three o'clock (London Waits) (i)	2'00"	Charles Wood	SATB						NJBC
63	U	196	Past three o'clock (London Waits) (ii)	3'00"	William Llewellyn	SSAATTBB	Br	2222	2231	Tp+2	Strings	NJBC
85		260	Puer Nobis (Unto us is born a Son)	2'00"	William Llewellyn	SATB		2222	2231	Tp+2	Strings	NJBC
64		200	Rejoice and be merry (A Gallery Carol)	1'30"	Robin Wells	SATB		2222	2231	Tp+2	Strings	NJBC
65		204	Rejoice lordings	0'50"	Arthur Oldham	SATB						
45	U	120	Rocking Carol (Mary's Child, so new and fair)	1'35"	William Llewellyn	SAATTBB						NJBC
54	U	160	Sans Day Carol (Now the holly bears a berry)	1'50"	Ian Humphris	SAATTBB						
44a	U	118	Sant Josep i la Mare (Mary, Mother of God's dear child)	1'30"	Père Jorda	SATB						
44b	U	119	Sant Josep i la Mare de Deu	1'30"	Père Jorda	SATB						
66	U	209	See him born (Il est né, le divin enfant)	2'00"	William Llewellyn	SSAATTBB		1200			Strings	NJBC
67	U	212	See, to us a child is born (A Christmas Antiphon) (i)	1'30"	John Wilson	SATB						
68	U	213	See, to us a child is born (A Christmas Antiphon) (ii)	1'30"	John Wilson/W. Ll.	SATB						
69	U	216	Silent night (Stille Nacht)	2'40"	Ian Humphris	SAATTBB						
70	U	218	Sing lullaby! (The Infant King)	1'45"	William Llewellyn	SATB						
50	U	140	Sir Christmas (Nowell, Nowell, Who is there?)	1'05"	Robin Wells	SATBB						
24	U	60	Slumber Song of the Madonna (Hushaby low)	2'00"	Ronald Finch	SAATTBB	S					
69	U	216	Stille Nacht (Silent night)	2'40"	Ian Humphris	SAATTBB						
4	U	6	Susanni (A little child there is yborn)	1'45"	Ronald Corp	SATB						
71	U	220	Sweet was the song the Virgin sang (Lute-book Lullaby)	2'15"	Jeremy Thurlow	SSAATTBB						
72	U	223	The angel Gabriel (Gabriel's message)	2'15"	William Llewellyn	SSATTBB		1200			Strings	NJBC
73	U	226	The Christ-child lay (Carol of the Christ-child)	1'30"	Philip Riley	SATB						
74	U	228	The first Nowell	4'30"	William Llewellyn	SATB		2222	2231	Tp+2	Strings	NJBC
53	U	156	The Golden Carol (Now is Christemas ycome)	1'10"	Paul Bendit	SSAATTBB						
76	U	234	The holly and the ivy	2'45"	William Llewellyn	SSAATTBB	ST	2222	2231	Tp+2	Strings	NJBC
70	U	218	The Infant King (Sing lullaby!)	1'45"	William Llewellyn	SATB						
5	U	9	The little road to Bethlehem (As I walked down the road)	3'00"	Michael Head	SSAATTBB						
77	U	236	The oak stands fast (The Trees of the Field)	1'20"	David Stone	SATB						

NO.	PAGE	U	TITLE AND FIRST LINE (both are shown)	TIME	COMPOSER OR ARRANGER	VOICES Minimum Choir	Solo	INSTRUMENTAL PARTS (on hire)				JUNIOR BOOK (NJBC)
								Wind	Brass	Perc.	Strings	
11	23		The Oxen (Christmas Eve)	2'30"	Benjamin Britten	SA						
78	238	U	There is no rose of such virtue	2'00"	John Joubert	SATB						
79	240	U	The Shepherds' Farewell (Thou must leave)	3'30"	Hector Berlioz	SATB		0220			Strings	
28a	72	U	The Song of the Birds (In this most joyful night)	3'00"	Enrique Ribo	SATB						
77	236	U	The Trees of the Field (The oak stands fast)	1'20"	David Stone	SATB						
61	187	U	The Twelve Days of Christmas (On the First day)	3'40"	Ian Humphris	SSAATTBB	SB					NJBC
87	266	U	The Yorkshire Wassail (Wassail! We've been awhile)	3'00"	Ian Humphris	SSAATTBB	S/A					
79	240	U	Thou must leave (The Shepherds' Farewell)	3'30"	Hector Berlioz	SATB		0220			Strings	
80	244		Torches! (i)	1'40"	John Joubert	S or SA		2222	4231	Tp+1	Strings	NJBC
81	247		Torches! (ii)	1'40"	John Joubert	SATB		2222	4231	Tp+1	Strings	NJBC
26	66	U	Troc-a-tron (I'm a-ridin' to Bethlehem)	0'50"	Petr Eben	SATB						
82	250	U	'Twas in the moon of wintertime (Huron Carol)	1'50"	William Llewellyn	SSAATTBB						
84	256	U	Tyrle, tyrlow	1'45"	Healey Willan	SSAA						
85	260		Unto us is born a Son (Puer Nobis)	2'00"	William Llewellyn	SATB		2222	2231	Tp+2	Strings	NJBC
86	264		Villagers all, this frosty tide (Joy shall be yours)	1'30"	H. Fraser-Simson	SATB						
87	266	U	Wassail! We've been awhile (The Yorkshire Wassail)	3'00"	Ian Humphris	SSAATTBB	S/A					
83	253	U	What shall we give? (El Noi de la Mare)	1'50"	Enrique Ribo	SSAATTBB	S					
89	272	U	Whence is that goodly fragrance flowing? (i)	2'15"	William Llewellyn	TTBBB	T					
90	274	U	Whence is that goodly fragrance flowing? (ii)	2'15"	Robin Wells	SSATTBB						
88	270	U	Worship the Christ-child (Canon for three choirs)	1'30"	W. A. Mozart/W. Ll.	[SATB]×3						